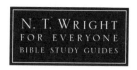

N. T. WRIGHT
FOR EVERYONE
BIBLE STUDY GUIDES

1 & 2 TIMOTHY AND TITUS

12 STUDIES FOR INDIVIDUALS AND GROUPS

N. T. WRIGHT

WITH PHYLLIS J. LE PEAU

IVP Connect

An imprint of InterVarsity Press
Downers Grove, Illinois

Kathy

InterVarsity Press
P.O. Box 1400, Downers Grove, IL 60515-1426
World Wide Web: www.ivpress.com
E-mail: email@ivpress.com

InterVarsity Press® is the book-publishing division of InterVarsity Christian Fellowship/USA®,
a movement of students and faculty active on campus at hundreds of universities, colleges and schools
of nursing in the United States of America, and a member movement of the International Fellowship of
Evangelical Students. For information about local and regional activities, write Public Relations Dept.,
InterVarsity Christian Fellowship/USA, 6400 Schroeder Rd., P.O. Box 7895, Madison, WI 53707-7895,
or visit the IVCF website at <www.intervarsity.org>.

Cover design: Cindy Kiple
Cover image: Adam Hall/Trevillion Images

ISBN 978-0-8308-2194-5

Printed in the United States of America ∞

P   18   17   16   15   14   13   12   11   10   9   8   7   6   5   4

Y   24   23   22   21   20   19   18   17   16   15

CONTENTS

Getting the Most Out of 1 & 2 Timothy and Titus

Taken together, 1 and 2 Timothy and Titus are usually called "the Pastoral Letters," partly because Paul is acting as a pastor to Timothy and Titus, and partly because he is writing to instruct them in their own pastoral ministries and in the ministries that they are to establish in their various congregations. But they might equally be called "the Teacher's Manual," because so much of what they contain is about the kind of teaching that Christian leaders should be giving—and, just as much, the kind they shouldn't.

These letters are concerned with two types of teaching. We shall see Paul come back to them from several different angles in these three letters. One type of teaching, which he warns against, goes round and round in circles, picking up interesting ideas and theories and playing with them endlessly. This leads to confusion with no clear understanding or guidance. The other has a clear aim, cuts out anything that gets in the way of it and goes straight to the point.

The teaching of the gospel itself, and of the way of life which flows from it, must not be a muddled, rambling thing, going this way and that over all kinds of complex issues. It must go straight to the point and make it clearly, so that the young Christians who so badly need building up in their faith may learn the deep, rich, basic elements of Christian teaching. These are what make genuine Christianity stand out from the world around it, and they should not be hidden under a thick casing of complex and impenetrable ideas.

We are told clearly that the teaching in these letters does not aim at just conveying information, but a whole way of life summed up in 1 Timothy 1:5—one of love, which comes from a pure heart and a good conscience and a sincere faith.

Underneath these we can detect two concerns which run through these letters. First, Paul is anxious that everyone who professed Christian faith should allow the gospel to transform the whole of their lives, so that the outward signs of the faith express a living reality that comes from the deepest parts of the personality. Second, he is also anxious that each Christian, and especially every teacher of the faith, should know how to build up the community in mutual love and support rather than, by the wrong sort of teaching or behavior, tearing it apart.

We know even today, with two thousand years of history, how easily things can seem to fall apart. As we study through this guide (prepared with the help of Phyllis Le Peau, for which I am grateful) we will see how much more fragile the little churches must have seemed in those early days, with tiny communities facing huge problems.

But, as the opening greeting insists, they do not face those problems alone and neither do we. As was true for Paul's apostleship, our ministry and life in Christ are rooted in God's command. (For more background and reflection on these letters see my *Paul for Everyone: The Pastoral Letters*, on which this guide is based, published by SPCK and Westminster John Knox.)

As we study 1 and 2 Timothy and Titus, we too can be assured, even as Paul assured Timothy, of God's grace, mercy and peace.

SUGGESTIONS FOR INDIVIDUAL STUDY

1. As you begin each study, pray that God will speak to you through his Word.

2. Read the introduction to the study and respond to the "Open" ques-

tion that follows it. This is designed to help you get into the theme of the study.

3. Read and reread the Bible passage to be studied. Each study is designed to help you consider the meaning of the passage in its context. The commentary and questions in this guide are based on my own translation of each passage found in the companion volume to this guide in the For Everyone series on the New Testament (published by SPCK and Westminster John Knox).

4. Write your answers to the questions in the spaces provided or in a personal journal. Each study includes three types of questions: observation questions, which ask about the basic facts in the passage; interpretation questions, which delve into the meaning of the passage; and application questions, which help you discover the implications of the text for growing in Christ. Writing out your responses can bring clarity and deeper understanding of yourself and of God's Word.

5. Each session features selected comments from the For Everyone series. These notes provide further biblical and cultural background and contextual information. They are designed not to answer the questions for you but to help you along as you study the Bible for yourself. For even more reflections on each passage, you may wish to have on hand a copy of the companion volume from the For Everyone series as you work through this study guide.

6. Use the guidelines in the "Pray" section to focus on God, thanking him for what you have learned and praying about the applications that have come to mind.

SUGGESTIONS FOR GROUP MEMBERS

1. Come to the study prepared. Follow the suggestions for individual study mentioned above. You will find that careful preparation will greatly enrich your time spent in group discussion.

2. Be willing to participate in the discussion. The leader of your group will not be lecturing. Instead, she or he will be asking the questions

found in this guide and encouraging the members of the group to discuss what they have learned.

3. Stick to the topic being discussed. These studies focus on a particular passage of Scripture. Only rarely should you refer to other portions of the Bible or outside sources. This allows for everyone to participate on equal ground and for in-depth study.

4. Be sensitive to the other members of the group. Listen attentively when they describe what they have learned. You may be surprised by their insights! Each question assumes a variety of answers. Many questions do not have "right" answers, particularly questions that aim at meaning or application. Instead the questions push us to explore the passage more thoroughly.

    When possible, link what you say to the comments of others. Also, be affirming whenever you can. This will encourage some of the more hesitant members of the group to participate.

5. Be careful not to dominate the discussion. We are sometimes so eager to express our thoughts that we leave too little opportunity for others to respond. By all means participate! But allow others to also.

6. Expect God to teach you through the passage being discussed and through the other members of the group. Pray that you will have an enjoyable and profitable time together, but also that as a result of the study you will find ways that you can take action individually and/or as a group.

7. It will be helpful for groups to follow a few basic guidelines. These guidelines, which you may wish to adapt to your situation, should be read at the beginning of the first session.

    • Anything said in the group is considered confidential and will not be discussed outside the group unless specific permission is given to do so.

    • We will provide time for each person present to talk if he or she feels comfortable doing so.

- We will talk about ourselves and our own situations, avoiding conversation about other people.
- We will listen attentively to each other.
- We will be very cautious about giving advice.

Additional suggestions for the group leader can be found at the back of the guide.

PAUL AS AN EXAMPLE OF GOD'S SAVING GRACE

1 Timothy 1

In the old radio and TV series *The Lone Ranger*, Silver, The Lone Ranger's horse, became almost as famous as the man himself. When we first meet Silver, the horse is not only unbroken and untamed but is assumed to be unbreakable, untamable. But The Lone Ranger is not to be put off. By some secret means he calls the animal to be his, and the horse responds and gives him a lifetime of service.

From the moment The Lone Ranger shows that he can tame the untamable horse and make it into his servant, and even in a measure his friend, the viewer knows he will be able to conquer all the other obstacles in his path. After all, he has already accomplished the hardest task.

This is precisely the point that Paul is making when he talks of what God has done in his life. God has taken the wildest, most violent of blaspheming persecutors, and has transformed him into not only a believer but a trusted apostle and evangelist. If God can do that, there is nobody out there—no heart so hard, no anger so bitter—who remains outside the reach of God's patient mercy.

OPEN

When have you been surprised by receiving unexpected grace from someone? What was it like?

STUDY

1. *Read 1 Timothy 1:1-20.* Paul, once a violent and feared enemy of Christians but now an apostle of King Jesus, writes to his spiritual son Timothy. What is Paul's charge to Timothy?

   To give grace, mercy & peace.
   Keep faith & clear conscience

2. How does Paul sum up a whole way of life in 1:5?

3. As the opening greeting insists, Paul and Timothy do not face their task alone. Paul's apostleship is rooted in God's command to him, and he assures Timothy of God's grace, mercy and peace. The God he invokes is the Savior—a title often used in the first century for the Roman emperor, the caesar of the day—and the Jesus he follows as his hope is the King, the Messiah, the world's true Lord.

   Paul says some people had been sidetracked by myths, endless genealogies, disputes and foolish talk (vv. 4-6). What can sidetrack us from the core elements of the Christian faith?

   Doing things always the same
   way — accepting people where
   they are —

4. Paul states that some people have wandered from the faith and want to be teachers of the law but don't understand what they are talking about. What is the purpose of the law (vv. 8-10)?

5. The Jewish law is like a map which only marks danger. It only tells us where we should not go. For such a purpose the law is very useful. But it will not tell you what you should do. (See vv. 8-11.)

Teaching from gospel - good news

How does the law contrast with the healthy teaching of the gospel?

6. This gospel was entrusted to Paul. Contrast Paul's life before his conversion with his life after his conversion (vv. 12-15).

spoke evil, persecuted + insulted Christ
He got grace, faith + love God was merciful

7. Why did Paul receive such mercy from God (vv. 15-16)?

Jesus came into world to save sinners

8. What difference does it make to us that a person like Paul received such mercy?

We, then can also feel the grace + mercy of God's love.

9. As happens so often in Paul's writings, the passage which seemed to be all about Paul is in reality all about God and his grace and love. So it's quite appropriate that Paul ends it with an outburst of praise to the one true God (v. 17).

    How can praise and worship of the one true God be more a part of your life? *Realizing God is always with us*

10. What is Paul's command to Timothy in verses 18-19?
    Keep faith & clear conscience

11. How are both faith and a good conscience necessary to live as God desires?

12. Because Hymenaeus and Alexander (v. 20) did not have a moral compass (a conscience educated and guided by the Spirit of Christ), their faith ended up shipwrecked, and so they were put out of the Christian assembly.

    What can aid us in holding on to faith and a good conscience?
    Praying

PRAY

Offer praise to God for the ways he has shown mercy to you.

2

PRAYER,
MEN AND WOMEN

1 Timothy 2

When we pray, most of us would start with the people we know and love best: our spouse, our children, our parents; other close relatives; friends we see frequently, who are uppermost in our minds; people facing illness or death. Prayer lists often go out in concentric circles, with ourselves in the middle—and we will be sure, no doubt, to pray for all the various concerns that hammer away at us in *our* own lives, *our* work, *our* responsibilities, *our* worries.

OPEN

What were the first names you wrote down the last time you made a prayer list?

STUDY

1. *Read 1 Timothy 2:1-7.* Paul prays for his friends and relatives, of

course; we know that from things he says over and over. But in this passage he strongly urges that we should start, as it were, at the other end.

For whom and what kinds of prayers does Paul suggest God's people should pray?

2. What reasons are given for praying for those in authority?

3. What does praying for those in government offices around the world have to do with people being saved and coming to know the truth?

4. For many Christians, particularly those of us who have grown up in the Western world and have never known war or major civil disturbance in our own country, praying for our leaders often seems quite remote. We might grumble about our leaders or some of their policies, but what they do doesn't drive us to our knees to pray for them, to beseech God to guide them and lead them to create a better world for all of us to live in.

Do you pray for those in high office? Why or why not?

5. Christians who live in countries with unstable or oppressive governments dread the knock on the door after dark which means that the secret police have come to take someone away, perhaps to be tortured or killed. They pray desperately for good, strong, wise, just rulers. They want leaders who will hold their world together and prevent the bullies and the cynical power-seekers from having it all their own way.

As happens so often in the New Testament, the call to prayer is also the call to think: to think clearly about God and the world, and God's project for the whole human race. Don't rest content with the simplistic agendas of the world that suggest you should either idolize your present political system or be working to overthrow it.

Take several minutes now to pray for rulers at home and around the world.

As we pray and watch what God will do in our society and the world, how might our own attitudes grow, change and mature?

6. *Read 1 Timothy 2:8-15.* A kind of war has been going on, in Western culture at least, for the last generation. It's been dubbed "the war of the sexes," though it's not so much a battle between men and women as it is between different visions of what the roles of the two sexes should be in society, in marriage and in the church. Life becomes confusing at this point: some men are very much in favor of equal rights for women, while some women are opposed to it. Passions run high. Those who grow up while it's all going on will discover soon enough that there are various parts of the traditional culture which are like unexploded land mines. Pick them up and they may go off in your hand. This passage could be one such bomb, ready to go off at a moment's notice.

According to this passage, what are men and women supposed to be like (vv. 8-10)?

7. In verse 8 Paul says men should pray everywhere without anger or disputing. How would this stand in contrast to the stereotypical image of men in Paul's day (and ours)?

8. What does it means for women to adorn themselves with good works?

9. I would translate verses 11-12 as: "They [women] must be allowed to study undisturbed, in full submission to God. I'm not saying that women should teach men, or try to dictate to them; rather, that they should be left undisturbed." This is remarkable in that it was unusual in Paul's day to say that women should be allowed to study.

   What's the value to men and women in having women be able to study?

10. Verse 12, which is often quoted as evidence that women should not speak, teach or lead in the church, need not be read as "I do not allow a woman to teach or hold authority over a man" (the translation

which has caused so much difficulty in recent years). It can equally mean "I don't mean to imply that I'm now setting up women as the new authority over men in the same way that previously men held authority over women."

Why might Paul need to say this to Timothy while he was in a place like Ephesus where the biggest temple housed a female-only cult to Artemis (or Diana as the Romans called her) in which the priests were all women?

While many whom I respect disagree about what these verses mean and how they should be applied, I believe the apostle was saying that on the one hand women should be trained and educated in the faith (in contrast to much of the Roman Empire), but that on the other hand Christianity should not become a cult like that of Artemis in Ephesus, where women did the leading and kept the men in line. Men should not lord it over women, nor women over men.

What are the advantages of a body of believers where men and women are encouraged to develop whatever gifts God has given them?

How do you respond to the perspective that Paul is calling both men and women to live in contrast to the standard images of male and female in the Roman world?

11. How might Christians today live in contrast to the standard images of male and female in our present world?

Let's not leave any more unexploded bombs and mines around for people to blow their minds with. Let's read this text as I believe it was intended, as a way of building up God's church, men and women, women and men alike. Just as Paul was concerned to apply this in one particular situation, so we must think and pray carefully about where our own cultures, prejudices and angers are taking us. We must do our best to conform, not to any of the different stereotypes the world offers, but to the healing, liberating, humanizing message of the gospel of Jesus.

PRAY

Ask the Holy Spirit to open your heart to the complexity of the truth in this passage, to change your thinking where it needs to change and to help you to live out what you have learned.

NOTE ON 1 TIMOTHY 2:13-15

I would translate these verses: "Adam was created first, you see, and then Eve; and Adam was not deceived, but the woman was deceived, and fell into trespass. She will, however, be kept safe through the process of childbirth, if she continues in faith, love and holiness with prudence."

What is Paul's point about Adam and Eve? Remember that his basic thrust is to insist that women, too, must be allowed to learn and study as Christians, and not be kept in unlettered, uneducated boredom and drudgery. Well, the story of Adam and Eve makes the point: look what happened when Eve was deceived. Women need to learn just as much as men do. Adam, after all, sinned quite deliberately; he knew what he was doing, he knew that it was wrong, and he deliberately went ahead. The

Old Testament is very stern about that kind of action.

What about the bit about childbirth? Paul doesn't see it as a punishment. Rather, he offers an assurance that, though childbirth is indeed difficult, painful and dangerous, often the most testing moment in a woman's life, this is not a curse which must be taken as a sign of God's displeasure. God's salvation is promised to all, women and men alike, who follow Jesus in faith, love, holiness and prudence. And that includes those who contribute to God's creation through childbearing.

3

The Character of Bishops and Deacons

1 Timothy 3

We had just begun to taxi out to the runway when suddenly the plane stopped. "Sorry, folks," the captain said. "Just got word. There's a small electrical fault. It's nothing serious but we have to fix it. We've got to go back to the gate and call the technician. Should be about twenty minutes."

Well, the twenty minutes turned into an hour, and eventually the frustrated passengers were invited to leave the plane, go back into the terminal and have a free drink at the café. I was struck by the absolute rule about turning back for even a minor fault. It wouldn't have affected the flight. It wouldn't have made the plane unsafe. But I would much rather err on the side of appropriate caution, even when it means the anticlimax of going back to the same airport lounge you left two hours earlier.

It set me thinking about some of the things in church life about which the New Testament tells us we should regularly be running checks. Like the character of church leaders, for instance.

OPEN

When you consider a candidate for national leadership, what characteristics are important to you?

STUDY

1. *Read 1 Timothy 3:1-16.* Paul says Christian leaders should be beyond reproach, so no one could lodge any accusation about their behavior (vv. 2, 10). What kind of complaints do people often make against Christian leaders?

2. In what areas does Paul say Christian leaders should strive for the highest standards (vv. 2-6, 8-12)?

3. How are typical expectations of behavior challenged by the gospel and these standards?

4. The life of a leader as described in this passage is a way of life which Paul expects outsiders to acknowledge as worthy. Many non-Christians will recognize when someone is living with the integrity proper to a faith in the living God, and respect them for it—and they will notice likewise when it isn't the case. How much attention do those

outside the church pay to Christian leaders? Give some examples.

5. Is Paul saying that there is one set of standards of behavior for leaders and another for everyone else? Explain.

6. Up to this point in this study we have considered the character of bishops and deacons, the leaders of the church. In these last verses we look more closely at the church. According to verse 15, what is the church?

7. How does Paul get across the idea that members of the church should show the same character and behavior as its leaders (v. 15)?

8. How do you respond to this idea?

9. Today we think of the meaning of the word *mystery* to be something for which there is "no explanation." That is, indeed, not far from the meaning the word had for people in Paul's day (the Greek word he uses is effectively the same, *mysterion*). In many of the popular

religions in Paul's world the idea of a "mystery" was something that *most* people couldn't and didn't understand, but that some did—though they of course kept it a secret so that everyone else would stay in the dark.

The Christian "religion" was different. It was a mystery, but one revealed to everyone. It was the fulfillment of the promises made by the One True God to Israel. Ponder verse 16. What do you understand of the mystery of godliness from this verse?

10. The point of it all in the present passage is that people who base their lives on this strange but powerful "mystery," people who allow their own personal story to be reshaped around the story of Jesus himself, discover that they are "the assembly of the living God," as opposed to the various gatherings of the "gods" of popular culture.

As you look over the whole chapter, whether you are a leader in the church or not, what stands out to you about the way you should "behave in God's household"?

PRAY

Pray for the leaders in your church, that the character described in this passage will be being built into them. Then ask the Lord to do the same for you.

Ask the Holy Spirit to impress upon you and your Christian community the power of the mystery of godliness. Pray that that power would be lived out in you and in your church as "the assembly of the living God."

4

PAY ATTENTION TO YOURSELF AND YOUR TEACHING

1 Timothy 4

Those called to Christian ministry may well feel that their task is never to think of themselves. There's a world out there, there's a church out there, and we are simply its servants. That is of course true at one level, as many passages in the New Testament insist. But at the same time one of the major problems in the church over the last few decades has been clergy burnout—a vivid and nasty metaphor for the horrible reality of combined physical exhaustion, emotional distress (feeling you have let everyone down), family disaster (overworked clergy sometimes ignore their family until it is too late), the possibility of losing your job, and, not least, the sense that you ought to be setting the church a good example but you're doing the opposite.

Faced with this problem, our present passage gives clear, strong and wise advice. "Give attention to reading, to exhortation and to teaching." "Don't neglect the gift that is in you." "Pay attention to yourself and your teaching." Each of these is important, and easily overlooked when you are under pressure.

OPEN

How do you respond to the idea "pay attention to yourself"?

Take care of your physical, mental & emotional needs. If you don't you may be of no use to anyone.

STUDY

1. *Read 1 Timothy 4:1-16.* How does Paul describe what will happen in the last times?

   Some people abandon the faith

2. What do you think it means that false teachers' consciences were branded with a hot iron?

   Following a false teaching

3. In the early church, and in many parts of Christianity, there were some whose experience of the pagan world had been very destructive. In particular, they had been used to engaging in wild and profligate sex, drunken orgies of various kinds. Modern as well as ancient experience suggest that when people go in for that kind of behavior in a serious way it turns out to be destructive, and they know in their bones that this is not how humans were made to live. Something in you dies when you give yourself indiscriminately to gluttony, whether in food, drink or sex. We can understand that some people who go that route may well end up hating the very thought of good food, of alcoholic drinks, or indeed of sex. For people like that, their inner guiding light which ought to tell them that some things are good and others aren't has been so mistreated that it now winces

at and reacts against even things which are perfectly good aspects of
God's good creation.

How do we see this problem reappearing today?

*Some people go off the deep end &
then think everything is bad.*

4. Why does Paul say everything God created is good and should be
received with thanksgiving (vv. 4-5)?

*Everything in moderation -
food, sex or whatever.*

Thanksgiving is more than just a recognition of the fact that we receive everything from the hands of a loving God. It is the fundamen-
tal human and Christian stance, poised between God and creation.
It simultaneously renounces idolatry (treating the created order as
if it were itself divine) and the notion that everything in creation is
shabby or bad. When we thank God we grow to our proper stature.
That's why those who reject creation, just like those who idolize it,
must be seen as deceitful and even demonic (v. 1). Finding our way
down the straight path between worshiping creation and rejecting
it may be difficult from time to time. But thanksgiving—coupling
God's word, which affirms the goodness of creation, with a grateful
prayer—is the key to it all.

5. How does training in godliness compare and contrast to training
physically?

*You need to practice each every
day*

Training in godliness is emphatically not what people today expect or want to hear. We expect and want to be told that "spirituality" is simply the sense I have of being in God's presence, being surrounded with his love, sensing a transcendent dimension in the affairs of everyday life. It comes as a shock to be told that it's something you have to work at—and something, moreover, which will take the same kind of hard work as going into training for athletics.

6. How do you train in godliness?

Prayer, actions, generosity

7. What is the purpose for and the outcome of this training in godliness (v. 10)?

Placed our hope in the living God, savior of all

8. What instructions are given to Timothy in verses 11-16?

(1) Don't let anyone look down
(2) Be an example
(3) read scripture
(4) preach & teach
(5) spiritual gifts

9. Which of these instructions do you find easy to follow and which are difficult? Explain.

read, preach & teach

10. What steps could you take to shore up those areas of weakness?

11. In verse 16 we are told to "pay attention to yourself." What kind of a person are you becoming?

Growing in compassion, service, love, generosity

Are you like someone giving classes on car maintenance while driving around a dangerous, battered old banger? Are you like a music teacher too busy to tune your own violin? Are you like the leader of a mountain expedition who's forgotten to bring your own walking boots? Of course there is a danger of being obsessed with yourself. Of course some people today spend too much time navel-gazing. For most of us that's not the problem. "Give attention." "Be diligent." "Pay attention." All these commands sound threatening. But once you see what they're saying, they are in fact liberating. Go ahead! Embrace and enjoy the true freedom of serving God and his people.

PRAY

Spend time in silent reflection paying attention to yourself. Now talk to God about what you see and feel. Turn over to him specific areas where you want to grow and be changed by him. Is your conscience in any way branded with a hot iron? If so, ask God how you should respond. In what ways are you struggling as you train in godliness?

Thank God for the gifts that he has given you. Recommit yourself to using those gifts for the kingdom of God.

Praise him for all the good things he has created for you to enjoy. Thank him that you are "fearfully and wonderfully made," more fascinating—dare we say more precious?—than anything else yet discovered in our world.

NOTE ON 1 TIMOTHY 4:10

Paul says that God is "the savior of all people—more especially, of believers." This has given rise to three different interpretations. Some think

Paul is saying that everyone will be "saved," in the full, final sense, but that those who believe the gospel in the present already enjoy salvation here and now, and so have a fuller "salvation" than those who don't.

Others, recognizing that Paul regularly warns that some will *not* be saved at the last, think that he's saying only that God is in principle, and potentially, the "savior" for everyone. In other words, anyone who wants to be saved will have to be saved by him rather than by someone else; but in fact the only people who are saved are believers.

Others again—and I think this is the best option—note that the word *savior* was in regular use in Paul's world as a title of honor for Caesar, the Roman emperor. In using it here for God (and for Jesus in 2 Timothy 1:10), Paul is claiming that this God and this Jesus are the true "savior" in the sense that through them the whole world will be rescued from decay and injustice. There is a sense in which the entire world is better off as a result of the saving work of God through Jesus. But since humans retain the right and dignity to refuse God's ultimate offer, it is only believers who appropriate this salvation fully.

5

RELATIONSHIPS: WIDOWS, ELDERS, SLAVES, MASTERS

1 Timothy 5:1—6:5

I know a wonderful couple who have eleven children. Mind you, they didn't have eleven together. His first wife died; her first husband died; they then met and married; and when they put his six and her five together, lo and behold, they had enough for a football team.

Imagine how you'd feel as one of the eleven. There are all kinds of new dynamics. Suddenly your family has more or less doubled in size, and you have to get used to being part of a household, doing regular chores, discovering one another's likes and dislikes, learning how to respect and value each other and not impose on or exploit one another. Extended families provide endless possibilities for tensions and difficulties as well as for friendship, fun and mutual support.

The early church did its best to live as a kind of extended family. In Paul's letters we find in various places the command to care for one another. This doesn't just mean thinking kind thoughts and saying comforting words. It means providing material and financial help for those in need.

OPEN

What was your family life like when you were growing up?

STUDY

1. *Read 1 Timothy 5:1-16.* There are several kinds of relationships covered in this passage. What guidelines are given about healthy family living within the church?

   Do what you can Respect, help

The reason that Paul is concerned about the church caring for others is directly and intimately related to his whole view of God, Jesus, the church and the world. It grows immediately out of his most central theological concerns. *The church is the renewed family of God, in the Messiah and in the power of the spirit;* and its family life must reflect that fact. Just because those of us in the modern West live in small family units with (for most of us) rather little contact with our fellow Christians, certainly by comparison with the early church, that shouldn't blind us to the reality of the extended Christian family that Paul was dealing with.

Christian theology, then, is closely bound up with guidelines for healthy family living.

2. What problems might creep in when these guidelines are not followed?

3. How can we balance the family life of all God's people with our responsibilities in our own families?

4. In 5:3-16 Paul speaks specifically about care of widows. In a world without any form of state-organized social welfare, the church from the very beginning took upon itself the task of caring for those with nobody to look after them and no means of supporting themselves. This meant, in particular, widows. In the ancient world, women whose husbands had died often faced total destitution. Often, when someone became a Christian, their own family would disown them, so that any support from relatives would be cut off. The church faced the task of living as an alternative family, and had to come to terms with the resulting tensions and difficulties, as well as the possibilities of joyful shared life and mutual support, especially in the context of likely having quite limited resources. This is why in this passage Paul goes into considerable detail on the rules for enrolling and supporting widows.

What problems is Paul trying to avoid by going into such detail on how to care for widows?

That the church wouldn't be overburdened.

5. How do these instructions relate to situations we face in our own day?

6. *Read 1 Timothy 5:17—6:5.* While many translations of 1 Timothy

5:17 read "double honor," the word most naturally refers in this passage to money, not to social respect. What might we learn in 5:17-18 about compensating our pastors?

We should be fair
& pay them on scale if
possible.

7. Why might Paul say an accusation against a pastor should be supported by two to three witnesses?

Because gossip & hearsay is
detrimental.

8. Why must a pastor avoid favoritism at all costs?

Because people don't want to
feel left out - bad feelings
come out of it.

9. What problems might occur from prematurely calling someone to ministry (5:22)?

10. Supposing the world goes on for another thousand years, and the Christians alive at that time look back at our generation, what would shock them most? Some would highlight how white Christians went along with the oppression of their black brothers and sisters; others would focus on the massive problem of debt in the Third World. Some will declare that Western Christianity has lost the plot entirely when it comes to sexual morality. It could be our unthinking use of oil-based products as a major energy source.

As we look back at the first century and ask "Why did they seem to tolerate that?" one of the biggest things that worries us about them would be their acceptance of slavery. Because all we can say about slavery is that it is wrong, we cannot believe that the early Christians did not have the same reaction.

The answer is, of course, that many of them did. But in Paul's day slaves formed up to one-third of the population. Most free families except the very poor owned at least one or two. Declaring grandly that you were opposed to the whole system would achieve about as much as someone today standing up in church and announcing that they were opposed to the use of oil-based products and therefore regarded cars, planes and motorized boats as unchristian. What the early Christians did, with Paul at their head, was to declare that masters and slaves were in fact equal before God (Galatians 3:28), and to treat both alike as possessing individual responsibility before God.

In 6:1-2 what attitude does Paul tell the slaves to have toward their masters? Why?

11. Where do you need to grow in respecting others who may not be seen by the world as your "equals" socially or economically?

12. What happens in Christian communities where the guidelines in this passage for community living are not followed (6:3-5)?

PRAY

Pray for your Christian community. Ask God to reveal to you unhealthy patterns that exist in you toward your community. Pray for unity that is honest and open, unity which deals with issues, and discipline that is needed. Pray that there will be confession of sin against each other and that forgiveness will be extended.

Thank God for the miracle of love and grace that can be experienced in community.

6

GODLINESS AND CONTENTMENT

1 Timothy 6:6-21

It is hardly an exaggeration to say that this famous passage is an indictment of modern Western culture. Never before in history has there been such a restless pursuit of riches, by more and more highly developed means. Never before has the love of money been elevated to the highest and greatest good, so that if someone asks you, "Why did you do that?" and you responded, "Because I could make more money that way," that would be the end of the conversation. Never before have so many people tripped over one another in their eagerness to get rich and thereby impaled themselves on the consequences of their own greed.

The greatest irony of it all is that it's done in the name of contentment—or, which is more or less same thing, happiness. Many people give lip service to the maxim that "money can't buy you happiness," but most give life-service to the hope that it just might, after all. Their "pursuit of happiness," and the idea that this is a basic human right, is all very well, but when it's taken to mean the unfettered pursuit of wealth it turns into a basic human wrong. And yet every advertisement, every other television program, many movies and most political manifestos are designed, by subtle and not-so-subtle ways, to make us say, "If only I had just a bit more money, then I would be content."

OPEN

Describe a time when you felt most content.

STUDY

1. *Read 1 Timothy 6:6-21.* How is contentment defined and explained in this passage? *Religion can make you rich. Being happy with what you have.*

2. What happens to those who fall into the trap of loving money? *pull them into trap of foolish & harmful desires - wander from faith into shallow existence.*

The point is that the present world, the created order in which we live, is full of all kinds of good things. We should enjoy them in their appropriate ways and, by thanking God for them, maintain the careful balance of neither worshiping the created world nor imagining that it's evil. But when money comes into the equation everything looks different. Money is not, as it stands, God's creation, but a human invention to make the exchange of goods easier and more flexible. The further it becomes removed from the goods themselves, and the more it becomes a "good" in itself, the closer we come to idolatry. A society which values wealth for its own sake—which is where the Western world has been for at least the last few decades—has forgotten something vital about being human. Money itself isn't evil; but, as verse 10 famously puts it, loving money is not only evil, it's the root of all evil.

3. According to this passage, what is to be our response to the temptation to love money? Why? *righteousness, godliness, faith, love, endurance & gentleness. — eternal life —*

4. How does the description of King Jesus encourage us as we seek a proper attitude toward money?

   He lives in the light

5. What are possible ways you should revise how you deal with money?

   Don't be so stingy —

6. How is the life described in verses 9-10 a stunning contrast to that described in verses 11-16?

   This whole way of life (vv. 11-16) encourages us to lift up our heads and to see where we are called to go, rather than looking around at the rest of the world and being consumed with jealousy for the material wealth that others have got. People who do that discover in the process that they are beginning, in the present, to live "the life of the coming age" (v. 12). That's why when the King of kings reveals his Son, they will be ready for him and will celebrate his royal appearing.

7. In verses 17-19, what instructions are given to those who are rich in this world? *Don't be proud / Believe in God / Rich in good works, generous / & ready to share*

8. Give examples of what it might look like for you to live this way.

Part of the point of this passage, highlighted in verse 17, is the uncertainty of riches. Not only can't you take it with you when you go, as verse 7 reminded us, but you can't be sure you're going to keep it while you are here. In a world increasingly dominated by money it seems almost indecent to mention it, but the New Testament, as is often the case, is severely practical and reminds us of facts our culture wants us to forget. Money comes and goes; God doesn't. Money can't be relied upon, and even those who have plenty of it discover all too soon that it doesn't buy them contentment.

9. What do you rely on money to do for you, and what do you rely on God for? *Pay bills, give, roof over my head, clothes, food - necessities God - helping me to do what is right - Open my heart, mind & pocketbook*

Do you think you have the balance right? Explain.
Sometimes

10. What is Paul getting at with the promise he makes about generosity?
You get back more than you give

We can't use money to buy our way to God's new world. But because God's Spirit is at work within us, we are commanded to live our lives in accord with the new world we have already entered by faith. When we reach the goal, the risen and glorious life in God's new world, we will discover that the life we have led in the Spirit, in obedience to God, is indeed preparing and shaping us for that new world.

This is so whatever our circumstances. If we are poor, our required obedience will be appropriate for our poverty. If we are rich, our obedience will be appropriate for our wealthy state—and it may mean giving it all away. The point in either case is not that one category has an unfair advantage, but that each, like artists in training, must carve their own statue from the block of marble they've been given, not from the next person's.

11. Paul concludes in verses 20 and 21 by warning against a movement of those who claim special knowledge (*gnosis* in Greek) about levels of spiritual beings and the layers of heaven. There are still books and teachers today who claim special spiritual secrets or hidden identities.

How can these ideas distract us from living as God intends us to now in the robustly physical world he has created?

PRAY

Commit your money matters to the Lord. Ask him to reveal to you where you are living a life of obedience in relationship to what you possess and where you need to change.

Commit your life to the Lord. Ask him to help you chase after justice, godliness, faith, love, patience and gentleness, to fight the noble fight of faith, and to get a grip on the life of the coming age.

Praise God, the blessed and only Sovereign One, the King of kings and Lord of lords. He is the only one who possesses immortality; he lives in unapproachable light; no human being has seen or can see him. To him be eternal honor and power. Amen.

— Mary Ann
  Karen
  Lynn
  Lane

7

REKINDLE THE GIFT

2 Timothy 1

There was snow outside, and the living room was cold when I came downstairs. I don't know why I'd woken up early, but I now shivered as I huddled on the sofa and waited for one of my parents to follow me downstairs. (I can't have been more than about seven or eight, I suppose.) Before long my father appeared, and began to work on the fireplace. He twisted some newspaper, laid some fresh sticks, placed coal around the edge and then, kneeling down, blew very gently at the base of the fire. He didn't need to use a match. He'd seen that the coal in the very bottom of the fireplace was still glowing, still just alight. As he blew, I watched in amazement at what seemed like magic. The coal glowed brighter and brighter, and then suddenly the newspaper burst into flame. Within a minute the sticks were alight, the fire was going, and the room began to warm up.

I am reminded of this when I hear Paul urging his young friend to rekindle God's gift, to bring it back into a blazing fire. Something is glowing there, deep down inside Timothy, and he must blow gently on it to bring it back into flame.

OPEN

What are the dangers and benefits of fire?

STUDY

1. *Read 2 Timothy 1:1-7.* In what ways has God equipped Timothy to be
   a servant of King Jesus? *sincere faith*
   power, love +
   self control

2. What are the dangers and benefits of power in a church?
   abuse of power
   benefit, - standing up for
   what is true + loving

3. Instead of a spirit of fear, Timothy was given a spirit of power, love
   and prudence (v. 7). How can these counter fear?
   By faith in God
   + persevering

4. In what ways have you seen God equip you to serve him and his
   people?

5. *Read 2 Timothy 1:8-18.* How might Paul's imprisonment be a source
   of shame for Timothy or others?
   people turned against him

Paul was in prison because what he had been doing and saying was
seen as an offense to the people in power. He was announcing a royal
message, a "gospel" which clashed head-on with the royal message on

which the Roman Empire was built: the announcement of Caesar as Lord, the promise of his power to save the world, the prospect of his royal appearance in a city or province that obeyed his rule. "Paul in prison" meant "Paul out of favor with the power-brokers of the day."

6. What do you see in this passage that would be an antidote to this temptation to be ashamed of the gospel?

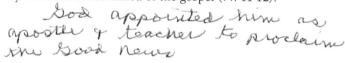

standing up & talking about what God says in the Bible

God's power overrides all earthly power. It has already been put to work in the call of the gospel which has transformed Paul and Timothy's own lives and is doing so for an increasing number of others as well. It will be put to work again when God makes the world anew and gives his people new life, new bodies, thus fulfilling the promise of life for which his people trust him in the present. This is the main theme of the passage: that if Timothy really understands the nature of God's power, he will learn to line up his sense of true honor and shame in relation to God himself, instead of in relation to the fickle, shifting and at best secondary earthly powers.

7. Why was Paul not ashamed of the gospel (vv. 11-12)?

God appointed him as apostle & teacher to proclaim the Good News

8. As Paul notes in verses 13-14, Christians are to commit themselves to God and the healthy pattern of teaching such as Paul provided, like someone putting their most precious possession into safe keeping in a bank or secure vault. But at the same time God commits something to us: a particular calling, a new set of responsibilities and ultimately the new life itself, the life we have in the present through the Spirit.

How are we to be faithful and responsible before God as he has been and is faithful to us?

Hold firmly to true words
remain in the faith & love
keep good things entrusted you

9. How does Paul contrast Phygelus and Hermogenes with Onesiphorus?

P & H deserted him
O stayed faithful to him.

10. Do you have someone you could describe as a soul friend? What difference would a soul friend like Onesiphorus make to you as you struggle to live out and proclaim the gospel?

11. As you consider this passage, what gift of the Spirit needs to be re-kindled in you?

PRAY

Ask the Holy Spirit to rekindle in you the gifts that he has given you. Ask him to renew you as you consider King Jesus and the power that raised him from the dead.

Praise God for the power of the gospel. Pray specifically for people in your life who need to know this power through a relationship with Jesus.

SERVING KING JESUS

2 Timothy 2

When I was at school, I shared a study for several terms with a friend. We got to know one another very well, the way you do when you find yourself in the same room, studying, meeting people, making coffee, snoozing over difficult tasks, worrying—or perhaps fantasizing—about the future and so on.

I dread to think what stories he could tell about me, and I could respond in kind. But one thing we both noticed about the other: we were both, at one stage, past masters at putting off as long as we could the daunting task of writing an essay. I would always know when he had difficult work to do: he would cut his nails, tidy his desk, rearrange his record collection and even sweep the floor. Anything to stave off for another moment, and then another, the challenge of creative thought and writing. Most of us, faced with a task we know will be demanding and difficult, find ways of avoiding it, even though we know we can't put it off forever.

Paul is warning Timothy against any such avoidance tactics when it comes to the central challenge of witnessing to the royal gospel of Jesus in the face of social and political stigma and danger.

OPEN

How do you usually respond to difficult or dreaded tasks?

- Try to explore the options
Ask people who have been
in similar situations,

STUDY

1. *Read 2 Timothy 2:1-13.* What instructions are given to Timothy in verses 1-3?

- Take teachings & entrust to reliable
people

- Take part in suffering

2. Why is it essential that the gospel be passed on?

People know they are
saved by grace.

This concern for continuity, for safe transmission of teaching, has sometimes been seen as a boring, conservative traditionalism, as though by simply saying the same thing, generation after generation, people would somehow be enlivened by the gospel. This is of course a caricature. The gospel which must be handed on is the most revolutionary message ever heard. Handing on the tradition safely is the only way to make sure that the next generation, too, is summoned whatever its costs to follow the radical gospel of King Jesus.

3. Paul uses three overlapping images, the soldier, the athlete and the farmer, to show what he means by "take your share of suffering" as one of King Jesus' soldiers. What insights do each of these images bring to the concept of suffering?

1. don't get mixed up in civilian life
2. obey rules
3. done part get 1st share

4. In light of those three images, in what ways have you suffered for the gospel?

5. According to verse 8, what is the gospel?

   Jesus raised from dead
   Descendant of David
   Good News

   How is this what you might expect, and how is it what you might not expect?

6. What is Paul getting at when he says that God's word is not tied up or chained (v. 9)?

   It is available to all
   who listen, study & believe

7. How do you experience the power of the Word of God in you and in the world around you?

   People's tolerance, patience,
   kindness

8. How are verses 11-13 both encouraging and troubling?

   If we deny him
   he also will deny us (?)
   If we are not faithful
   He remains faithful

Of course, there seems to be a discrepancy here. In one line Paul seems to say that denying Jesus brings terrible consequences and in the next that it doesn't after all. I don't think *faithless* here means "if we lose our faith," in the sense of ceasing to believe that Jesus is Lord and that God raised him from the dead. I think this is meant to take account of the fact that our faithfulness—our reliability, our stickability, our resolve, our determination to remain faithful in the sense of "loyal"—will waver and wobble from time to time. Those under intense pressure, whether political, spiritual, moral or whatever, will sometimes find themselves weak, faint and helpless. It is at those times that they need to learn a kind of second-order faith, a faith in the utter faithfulness and reliability of God himself, the God we know in and through Jesus, who was himself faithful to death. There is a world of difference between being blown off the ship's deck by a hurricane and voluntarily diving into the sea to avoid having to stay at the helm.

9. *Read 2 Timothy 2:14-26.* In verses 14-19 Paul talks about words. What is the difference between quarreling about words and carving out a straight path for the word of truth?

Arguing over trivial differences instead of viewing the whole picture.

When Paul talks about carving out a straight path for the word of truth, the picture he is most likely to have in mind is that of a pioneer hacking out a path through the jungle so that people can walk safely through. Part of the job of the teacher is to do what Paul himself is doing in this passage: to see where there are brambles, creepers and dead trees blocking the path which the word should be following to people's hearts and minds, and to shift them out of the way. This important work is in contrast to quarreling about words that don't matter and participating in empty chatter.

10. In verses 20-26 Paul offers another picture, the image of vessels in a great house with the promise that those who purify themselves from dishonorable things will become vessels of honor. How does Paul instruct Timothy to purify himself?

strive for righteousness, faith, love
& peace with a pure heart
call for help from God.

11. In what ways might you put these instructions into practice?

12. As you review this passage how would you like to grow as a servant of King Jesus?

Feeling worthy of the task

PRAY

Talk to Jesus about how you would like to more effectively serve him as your King.

STAND FIRM
IN THE SCRIPTURES

2 Timothy 3

It was a scrappy end to the game, but perhaps it was inevitable. We were winning by what should have been a safe margin; and with a few minutes to go the opposition seemed to realize that their cause was hopeless. Perhaps for that reason, though, they went berserk, as maybe only rugby players can. With nothing more to lose, they threw themselves about the place, fists swinging this way and that, boots flying out to trip or kick. They were furious that we'd won and they wanted to get some revenge in person even if they couldn't on the score line. I vividly remember the sigh of relief when the final whistle went and we all trooped off for a bath and to compare bruises.

OPEN

Think about a time when you were losing in a game or sports event and you knew you could not win. How did you feel and act?

STUDY

1. *Read 2 Timothy 3:1-9.* The early Christians staked their lives on their belief that with the death and resurrection of Jesus, God's new world had begun, so that the "last days" had indeed arrived, the interval between the defeat of evil on Calvary and the final defeat of evil that we still await.

   How does Paul describe the behavior of people in the last days?
   selfish, greedy, boastful, conceited insulting, disobedient, ungrateful unkind, violent, treacherous reckless

2. In what ways do you see these behaviors in people today?

3. As we look at the shocking list of behaviors, we must realize that seeds of each of them are hidden inside us as well. What seeds of these behaviors do you see in your own life or thinking?
   selfish

4. In what ways do people (including ourselves!) exhibit examples of legalism that keep a grip on the pattern of godliness but deny its power (v. 5)? *going to church, but not living its 10 commandments.*

5. Jannes and Jambres, according to ancient Jewish legend, were the two principal magicians of Egypt referred to in verses 11 and 22 of

Exodus 7. When Moses was performing the God-given signs to convince Pharaoh to let the Israelites go from their slavery, the Egyptian magicians did their best to copy the signs so that Pharaoh wouldn't take Moses seriously. Paul's point is that when the liberating, healing gospel is going forward in power, there will always be people who oppose it by whatever means and tricks they can.

Describe people (Christians or others) you have encountered like the ones Paul describes—people with strong agendas, convinced they are right, who approach people who can't say no and persuade them to join their cause, often targeting people whose troubled past and murky present make them easy targets for manipulation.

The poor in spirit, material possessions are who are targeted by t.v., politicians

6. If Jesus won a decisive victory over evil and death through his own death and resurrection, why do you think there is such a surge of evil in the world? *People don't believe doubt, fear, control*

7. *Read 2 Timothy 3:10-17.* As you reflect on this paragraph, what seems to have made the difference in Timothy's life?

followed teachings, conduct + purpose, observed faith, patience love + endurance, persecution + suffering

8. How have these influences been active (or not active) in your life?

9. How, according to Paul, is Scripture useful and what is its purpose?

    give wisdom to seek salvation
    teaches truth, instruction for
    right living –
        so we can do good

10. The word *breathed* that Paul uses in verse 16 is often translated "in-
    spired." But there are three ways people use with the word *inspired*
    today that are not helpful in understanding what Paul meant. First,
    people often speak of artists, poets, composers or even sports profes-
    sionals as being "inspired," something out of the ordinary that might
    give a boost to the spirits. Second, people sometimes mean that the
    minds of "inspired" poets went into neutral and some other force or
    spiritual source poured the words in from somewhere else. But nei-
    ther Jeremiah nor Paul nor the other writers of Scripture functioned
    as God's typewriters. Third, many equate the inspiration of Scripture
    with a particular theology that they know in advance to be true. Yet
    the Bible (rather than anyone's belief system) is breathed by God for
    the purpose of completing God's people for every good work.

    What particular passages of Scripture have changed you and pre-
    pared you to do what is right and good?

11. The Spirit speaking through Scripture can make us wise—and can
    help us think in new patterns, see things we hadn't seen before, un-
    derstand ourselves and other people and God and the world . . . and
    ultimately find ourselves rescued, saved, from the downward pull
    of sin and death, and transformed by God's forgiving grace so that
    we become part of his new creation. If we let Scripture have its way
    with us, all this is within reach, because, of course, Scripture not
    only unveils the living God we know in Jesus Christ, but, through
    our reading and pondering, it works this consciousness, by story,

poetry, symbol, history, theology and exhortation. Scripture not only gives us true information about how our lives can be transformed; it will itself be part of that process.

In what areas of your life do you want to be transformed by God through Scripture?

- finding peace of mind,
- acceptance of what happens
- finding ways to be fun, loving

12. What changes do you need to make for Scripture to be able to change you in these ways?

Heart + mind + soul open

PRAY

Ask God to permeate your heart, soul and mind with his Word. Consider what ways he might want Scripture to become more a part of your life.

WAITING FOR THE CROWN

2 Timothy 4

Paul lived his life with the clock ticking in the background, and he wants Timothy to do the same. Jesus is already enthroned as king of the world, and one day we shall see his royal appearing, the time when the whole world will be held to account. We don't know—we never know—how close to the final day we have come. But we are summoned to live each day, each year, as people ready to give account, ready to face scrutiny, assessment and judgment.

Paul compares this life to an athletic event. He wants us to picture ourselves in a stadium, perhaps even the amphitheater, for a gladiatorial contest. He has fought the fight, not an ordinary fight but the "good" or "noble" fight. He has run the course and stayed on track. That's why he then talks about the "crown," the badge which would be awarded to the winner, like an Olympic medal today.

OPEN

How do you feel when you watch Olympians being awarded their medals? How does this compare or contrast to what you feel when you receive a hard-earned reward?

STUDY

1. *Read 2 Timothy 4:1-22.* What is Paul's solemn charge to Timothy?

2. How does this charge compare with the tasks for which Paul said the Bible is useful in 1 Timothy 3?

3. When Paul tells Timothy to "announce the word" (v. 2), the New Testament hadn't yet been completely written or gathered into an authoritative collection, and he probably didn't have the Old Testament in mind. So what was he talking about when he said "the word"?

4. How do you and your Christian community announce the message of Jesus?

5. Paul says Timothy was to "rebuke, warn and encourage with all patience and explanation" (v. 2). How does this strike a helpful balance?

We probably all know people who inflict their own personality and opinions on everyone they meet, in a brash or even bullying way. Some Christians, alas, are like that, and sometimes justify their behavior by quoting texts like this. Each of us has to decide which category we fit into and hence which commands are appropriate for us.

6. In verses 3-4 Paul says that the time is coming when people will not tolerate healthy teaching. What evidence do you see of this intolerance?

People will not want the kind of teaching that will make them healthy and strong. Like people being instructed by their doctors to follow a particular diet, they will discover that half of their favorite foods aren't on it, and so will look for different doctors who will advise them to eat and drink what they like. In some parts of the Western world there are people who go from church to church trying to find preachers who will tell them what their ears are longing to hear.

Timothy must be aware of this danger, and must hold his course firmly. Verse 5 is a sober, realistic statement of what Christian ministry is about. You have received a particular calling: get on with it. Keep your balance. It may be difficult or painful at times, but you didn't sign on in order to have an easy life. Go on announcing Jesus as Lord. What is required is not success, as the world regards success, but loyalty and perseverance.

7. In the next paragraph Paul communicates how he has lived and is an excellent model for Timothy. He paints the pictures of one poured out as an offering, a fight, a race and receiving a crown. What do each of the pictures more fully describe regarding his ministry and life?

8. What concerns might some Christians have about God rewarding
   people?

The worry that many people have is related more particularly to the
doctrine of "justification by faith." Paul insists that our good works
will not justify us. Whenever he talks about the future, final judgment, on the great coming "Day of the Lord," he always speaks of it
as related not just to our faith, but to the total substance of our lives.
As with the logic of love, so with the logic of working for God in
the power of the Spirit: God retains the initiative, and remains the
ultimate source of energy, but Christians are called and required to
work hard with that energy. And when they do so, there will be an
appropriate reward.

9. Who is going to be rewarded on the final day?

10. How do you feel about the appearing of King Jesus himself?

11. As you review verses 9-22 what do you see is important to Paul?

The center of this rather scattered closing sequence shows Paul re-
flecting one more time on his task as the royal herald of King Jesus,

this time on the opportunity he had, when on trial for his life, to speak up for the message about his master. As he stood there in court, he was able to speak of Jesus as the Messiah, the world's true Lord, true King, and realized that he was being given a chance, perhaps a final one, to complete his work as Jesus' royal herald, this time with senior and influential non-Jews listening.

The picture we get, as we take leave of this intimate and personal letter, is of a man facing serious trouble and likely death, beset with problems and anxieties, but who nevertheless remains determined to bring every single aspect of his life into the orbit of the gospel itself, the royal proclamation of Jesus as Lord. He lives in the present world, Caesar's world, as already a cheerful citizen of the world to come, Jesus' world. He longs to see Timothy work hard and effectively for Jesus as he himself has done. And, as we listen in to his end of the conversation, we are left in no doubt as to what kind of advice he would give us today.

12. As you look back over the books of 1 and 2 Timothy, how have you been challenged to live your life worthy of the gospel?

PRAY

Talk to the Lord about what it means for you to faithfully serve and proclaim King Jesus.

GOD'S REVEALED PLAN

Titus 1

Children are aware, often with a sense of frustration, that there are basically two "ages," childhood and adulthood, and that they have to wait before they can attempt to turn their dreams into reality.

Deep within the mind and imagination of most first-century Jews lay the belief that world history itself is divided into two "ages": the present age and the age to come. There are several parallels between the way they thought about history and the way children see the future. *Now* we are frustrated, hemmed in by a world that isn't yet all that it will be. *Then* everything will be different; we shall be able to start our real life and show what we're made for. *Now* we, God's people, are being oppressed by wicked nations that don't know the true God, but worship idols and follow tyrannical leaders. *Then* we shall be free, and will share God's own rule of his glorious new world.

OPEN

Think of an experience in your life when you wished for "what was to come" instead of "what was at that time." Describe what it was like.

STUDY

1. *Read Titus 1:1-4.* How is God's character central to this passage?

2. In this introduction to his short letter, how does Paul place his ministry within the larger framework of God's overall plan?

3. One of the principal differences between Paul and those of his fellow Jews who didn't accept Jesus as the Messiah is that he believed that the future had come forward into the present, the *then* into the *now*, in the person of Jesus. That was the proclamation which he, Paul, was called upon to make. When he announced that God had raised Jesus from the dead, and installed him as King, Lord and Savior, he was introducing God's new age into the middle of the existing age.

    What difference does the promise that the life of the coming age has invaded the present age through Jesus make to you?

4. What is the significance of how Paul addresses Titus?

5. What has been your experience as a spiritual "child" or with having spiritual "children"?

6. *Read Titus 1:5-16.* Why are such specific instructions about the qualifications of elders important?

7. In what different areas of life must the elder be blameless? Why?

8. In what ways must he or she take initiative?

9. How seriously does the church today take choosing leaders?

The fashionable stance in today's Western world is against strong, clear teaching. People are suspicious of those who claim that we can be certain about some things. Many today prefer the flexible world where you can't be sure about anything and each of us has to find the way for ourselves. That has never been the Christian position, and it shouldn't be now.

Of course there are lots of things we can't be sure about. Of course there is new knowledge waiting to be discovered. Of course some of the things people thought they knew three hundred years ago must now be challenged, or expressed afresh. Nobody should doubt that. But equally there are many things upon which the church, and especially its leaders, must be clear and emphatic. Some of those who insist upon their certainties have done so in a bullying, stubborn fashion; that is of course ruled out by verse 7. But just because there is such a thing as arrogance doesn't mean there isn't such a thing as firm and well-grounded faith, expressed in loving clarity. May God give the church leaders who can teach like that.

10. What are the problems in Crete (vv. 10-16)?

11. What qualities of leaders from the previous paragraph are vital for ministering effectively in Crete?

Titus is not to compromise with such people. He isn't to soften Paul's hard line. Teaching like that is to be rejected from top to bottom, and people who hold it and propagate it won't be any use in building the community. Harsh words for hard realities. Applying all this will take courage. Titus has Paul's own example if he wants reminding of what that looks like in practice.

12. What does this passage say about the Western church today?

PRAY

Praise God that he has revealed his plan to us through Scripture. Praise him for how you are affected by that plan.

Now spend time praying for the leaders of your church. Use this passage as a guide for that prayer.

GOD'S KINDNESS
AND GENEROSITY

Titus 2—3

I went to a spectacular birthday party last weekend. Our host, who was turning seventy, had laid on a lavish evening. Nothing had been spared to make his guests comfortable and happy. The food was terrific, the wine of the highest class; each guest received a special little present, and the music and other entertainment kept us all excited and cheerful. At the end there were fireworks. We departed into the night filled with the warmth that comes from someone else's lavish generosity.

But supposing all the guests at the party were people who, not long before, had been critical of the host, or had plotted to do him down in his business, or had been the kind of people who never enjoyed parties, who didn't realize when someone was trying to be generous to them, and who certainly weren't used to saying "thank you." Supposing, nevertheless, that the host was determined to be generous, even to them. Why, you may ask, would anyone invite a bunch of miserable guests like that? Well, that's the question that faces us in this passage—because this, it appears, is precisely what God has done.

OPEN

When have you received a gift or kind act from someone whom you had mistreated or spoken unkindly of? How did you feel? How did you respond?

STUDY

1. *Read Titus 2:1—3:15*. Throughout this passage Paul tells Titus to instruct Christians to live according to healthy teaching and has much to say about the way they are to conduct themselves (2:1-10; 3:1-2, 8-11). What strikes you as important in these instructions? Why?

   self - control, sound in faith love + endurance, sober sincere + serious in teaching

2. Contrast the importance of the integrity of the family as shown in this passage with the attitude in the Western world today about the family. *women submitting to husbands (?)*

3. Why do you think Paul gives instructions about slavery when we would presume slavery to be wrong? *In the day slavery was accepted as a given.*

4. Throughout the passage Paul repeats the need for Christians to be ready or eager for and energetic about doing good works (2:7, 14; 3:1, 8, 14). Why is establishing a pattern of good works so important? *Start as children - learn to give*

We might understand the phrase, "good works" simply as "behaving yourself," but that is not the case. Nor are good works living a good moral life or obeying the law. They are the good works of giving practical help, particularly money, to those in need, or where there are social emergencies that require urgent assistance. When mentioned throughout this passage, the term "good works" refers to generous and helpful actions on behalf of the wider community.

In a sense that is what Christianity was. One of the remarkable things the early Christians were known for—and one of the reasons for the rapid spread of the faith—is the way they were unstoppable when it came to helping others, both financially and in practical ways. Having been gripped by the generous love of God themselves, they couldn't help acting in the same way.

People are watching us all the time.

5. What pattern of good works are you establishing in your life?

Giving money + time to help others.

6. According to verses 2:11-14 what is the basis of Paul's appeal about how Christians should live?

Jesus gave his life so we coued be saved —

7. The future-in-the-present has appeared, though not in the form of a dramatic new social experiment, nor in the shape of yet another oppressive regime stamping on everyone in its path, but in the form of the death and resurrection of Jesus. Paul doesn't mention this explicitly, but it's obviously what he has in mind in verse 2:11 when he talks about God's saving grace appearing for all people. The events of Jesus' life, death and resurrection were for him the moment when, and the means by which, the generous and powerful love of God

(that's what he means by "grace") were unveiled for the benefit, not of one group of people only, but of all the human race. With those brief but earth-shattering events, the future had been unveiled, and everything looked different as a result.

How should this glimpse of how life as it is going to be affect how you live now?

Try to live that life now.

8. As you look at 2:11-14, what might Paul's response be to someone who thinks that this lifestyle is too hard?

We must assume, then, that Titus isn't simply supposed to insist on certain styles of behavior for their own sake, or to exhort or warn people by the sheer force of his own personality. The way he is to insist on all this (2:15) is, as Paul himself has done, to explain to people how their present life relates to God's future, and to encourage them to make that future their own here and now.

9. Describe what we were once like according to 3:3.

selfish, foolish, disobedient & wrong. malice & envy

10. How was God's love, kindness and generosity lavished upon us?

He shows us mercy & love.

11. Take stock of yourself. How have you experienced the kindness and generosity of God?

Been blessed with good health, wonderful daughter

12. What difference is it making in your life?

13. As you look back over 1 and 2 Timothy and Titus, how would you like to become the person who more accurately reveals to the world who God is and what he is like?

Need to keep growing in faith, doing the best I can in all things.

PRAY

Praise God for lavishing his love and generosity upon you. Talk to him about how you want to live out this love and generosity to others.

NOTE ON TITUS 2:9-10

The commands to slaves in verses 2:9-10 are to be seen, of course, in the setting of ordinary daily life in the first century. Slavery was a fact of life and there was no point pretending it wasn't. You could no more abolish slavery overnight in the first century than you could invent space travel. The fact that you might hope it would happen one day, and wished it would, wouldn't justify giving slaves the impression that now they were Christians they could disobey their masters—any more than a futuristic fantasy about space travel would have justified Paul in selling tickets to Mars. The early Christians worked within what was possible at the time, while constantly lodging protests against abuses within the system and, where they could, against the system itself.

The vital thing was that slaves, having become Christians, shouldn't regard themselves as above the law. Some might think, "Because my master isn't a Christian, and I am, this gives me a right to tell him what's what—after all, I'm a servant of the King of the World and he isn't!" What message would that send to the watching world of Crete or anywhere else? It would indicate that this new cult was simply making trouble and ought to be stamped out. No: Christian slaves, like Christians in every walk of life, must be good advertisements, good ambassadors, for the teaching of God our Savior.

GUIDELINES FOR LEADERS

My grace is sufficient for you.
(2 Corinthians 12:9)

If leading a small group is something new for you, don't worry. These sessions are designed to flow naturally and be led easily. You may even find that the studies seem to lead themselves!

This study guide is flexible. You can use it with a variety of groups—students, professionals, coworkers, friends, neighborhood or church groups. Each study takes forty-five to sixty minutes in a group setting.

You don't need to be an expert on the Bible or a trained teacher to lead a small group. These guides are designed to facilitate a group's discussion, not a leader's presentation. Guiding group members to discover together what the Bible has to say and to listen together for God's guidance will help them remember much more than a lecture would.

There are some important facts to know about group dynamics and encouraging discussion. The suggestions listed below should equip you to effectively and enjoyably fulfill your role as leader.

PREPARING FOR THE STUDY

1. Ask God to help you understand and apply the passage in your own life. Unless this happens, you will not be prepared to lead others. Pray too for the various members of the group. Ask God to open

your hearts to the message of his Word and motivate you to action.

2. Read the introduction to the entire guide to get an overview of the topics that will be explored.

3. As you begin each study, read and reread the assigned Bible passage to familiarize yourself with it. This study guide is based on the For Everyone series on the New Testament (published by SPCK and Westminster John Knox). It will help you and the group if you have on hand a copy of the companion volume from the For Everyone series both for the translation of the passage found there and for further insight into the passage.

4. Carefully work through each question in the study. Spend time in meditation and reflection as you consider how to respond.

5. Write your thoughts and responses in the space provided in the study guide. This will help you to express your understanding of the passage clearly.

6. It may help to have a Bible dictionary handy. Use it to look up any unfamiliar words, names or places. The glossary at the end of each New Testament for Everyone commentary may likewise be helpful for keeping discussion moving.

7. Reflect seriously on how you need to apply the Scripture to your life. Remember that the group members will follow your lead in responding to the studies. They will not go any deeper than you do.

LEADING THE STUDY

1. At the beginning of your first time together, explain that these studies are meant to be discussions, not lectures. Encourage the members of the group to participate. However, do not put pressure on those who may be hesitant to speak—especially during the first few sessions.

2. Be sure that everyone in your group has a study guide. Encourage the group to prepare beforehand for each discussion by reading the introduction to the guide and by working through the questions in each study.

3. Begin each study on time. Open with prayer, asking God to help the group to understand and apply the passage.

4. Have a group member read aloud the introduction at the beginning of the discussion.

5. Discuss the "Open" question before the Bible passage is read. The "Open" question introduces the theme of the study and helps group members to begin to open up, and can reveal where our thoughts and feelings need to be transformed by Scripture. Reading the passage first will tend to color the honest reactions people would otherwise give—because they are, of course, supposed to think the way the Bible does. Encourage as many members as possible to respond to the "Open" question, and be ready to get the discussion going with your own response.

6. Have a group member read aloud the passage to be studied as indicated in the guide.

7. The study questions are designed to be read aloud just as they are written. You may, however, prefer to express them in your own words.

   There may be times when it is appropriate to deviate from the study guide. For example, a question may have already been answered. If so, move on to the next question. Or someone may raise an important question not covered in the guide. Take time to discuss it, but try to keep the group from going off on tangents.

8. Avoid answering your own questions. An eager group quickly becomes passive and silent if members think the leader will do most of the talking. If necessary repeat or rephrase the question until it is clearly understood, or refer to the commentary woven into the guide to clarify the context or meaning.

9. Don't be afraid of silence in response to the discussion questions. People may need time to think about the question before formulating their answers.

10. Don't be content with just one answer. Ask, "What do the rest of you think?" or "Anything else?" until several people have given answers to the question.

11. Try to be affirming whenever possible. Affirm participation. Never reject an answer; if it is clearly off-base, ask, "Which verse led you to that conclusion?" or again, "What do the rest of you think?"

12. Don't expect every answer to be addressed to you, even though this will probably happen at first. As group members become more at ease, they will begin to truly interact with each other. This is one sign of healthy discussion.

13. Don't be afraid of controversy. It can be very stimulating. If you don't resolve an issue completely, don't be frustrated. Explain that the group will move on and God may enlighten all of you in later sessions.

14. Periodically summarize what the group has said about the passage. This helps to draw together the various ideas mentioned and gives continuity to the study. But don't preach.

15. Conclude your time together with the prayer suggestion at the end of the study, adapting it to your group's particular needs as appropriate. Ask for God's help in following through on the applications you've identified.

16. End on time.

Many more suggestions and helps for studying a passage or guiding discussion can be found in *How to Lead a LifeGuide Bible Study* and *The Big Book on Small Groups* (both from InterVarsity Press/USA).